Presented to

_____

from

_____

on the occasion of

_____

Published by
**Lion Hudson Limited**
Wilkinson House, Jordan Hill Business Park,
Banbury Road, Oxford OX2 8DR, England
www.lionhudson.com

ISBN 978 1 85985 869 1
e-ISBN 978 1 78128 081 2

First edition 2013

**Acknowledgments**

Every effort has been made to trace and contact copyright owners.
We apologise for any inadvertent omissions or errors.

Authors can be found in the index of first lines.
All unattributed prayers by Karen Williamson are copyright © ZipAddress Limited

Psalm 23:1 (on page 80) is taken from The Authorized (King James) Version. Rights in the
Authorized Version are vested in the Crown. Reproduced by permission of the Crown's
patentee, Cambridge University Press.

The Lord's Prayer (on page 81) is adapted from the Holy Bible, New Living Translation,
copyright © 1996, 2004, 2007 by Tyndale House Foundation. Used by permission of
Tyndale House Publishers, Inc., Carol Stream, Illinois 60188. All rights reserved.

A catalogue record for this book is available from the British Library

Printed and bound in China, November 2018, LH54

# My Little Prayers

Karen Williamson
Illustrated by Amanda Enright

CANDLE
BOOKS

# Contents

Praise God!  7

A new day!  10

At school  11

Dinner time  15

Thank you  19

Travels  26

Quiet times  28

Please, God  33

My friend Jesus  36

When I'm scared...  38

All the people I love  39

God's wonderful world  46

Sorry! 51

Children, everywhere 54

Birthdays 56

Harvest 58

Christmas 61

Easter 64

At the end of the day 67

Bedtime 73

Through the night 79

The Lord's Prayer 81

An old prayer 82

Index of First Lines 83

# Praise God!

Dear God,
I feel like praising you.
I like singing to you at the
  top of my voice!
Thank you for everything!

Give me joy in my heart,
Keep me praising,
Give me joy in my heart, I pray;
Give me joy in my heart,
Keep me praising
Till the break of day.

Praise him, praise him,
Everybody praise him —
God is love, God is love!

# A new day!

Dear Lord Jesus,
We have this day only once.
Before it goes,
help us to do the good we can,
so it's not wasted.

# At school

Dear Lord,
I am starting my new school tomorrow.
I'm really scared.
There are big butterflies in my tummy.
Please come to school with me
and help me make new friends.
Thank you, Lord.

Heavenly Father,
Thank you for our school.
My teacher is really kind and helpful.
She's good at explaining things to me.
Thank you for my teacher, Lord.
Our lessons are a lot of fun.
I really enjoy learning things.

Dear Jesus,
Please help me at school.
Sometimes I find it hard,
and then I specially need you to help me.
Amen

Dear Lord Jesus,
Please help me to be brave.
I'm scared of lots of things.
I'm scared of big boys in the playground.
I'm scared of our friends' dog.
Please take away my fears.
Thank you, God.

# Dinner time

Thank you for the world so sweet,
Thank you for the food we eat,
Thank you for the birds that sing,
Thank you, God, for everything.

Heavenly Father,
Thank you for our daily food.
Our tummies are always full!
Please help the poor children we see on TV
who don't get enough to eat everyday.

God is great, God is good.
Let us thank him for our food.
By his hands, we are fed.
Let us thank him for our bread.
Amen

God, we thank you for this food,
For rest and home and all things good;
For wind and rain and sun above,
But most of all for those we love.

# Thank you

God made the sun,
God made the trees,
God made the mountains,
And God made me.

Thank you, God,
For the sun and the trees,
For making the mountains,
And for making me.

Dear Lord,
Thank you for music.
I love hearing happy songs
– and singing them, too.
Thank you for giving us music,
Lord.

Hooray!
You made the giraffe as tall as a tree.
Thank you, God.
Hooray!
You made the caterpillar, ant, and bee.
Thank you, God.
Hooray!
You made our world so perfectly.
Thank you, God.

Dear God,
Thank you for giving us the Bible,
so we can learn about you.
Amen

Dear God,
You know all about me.
You know the colour of my eyes.
You know what I most like to eat.
You know when I'm happy or sad.
And you know what's best for me.
Thank you, Lord.

Dear Lord,
I saw a beautiful rainbow this afternoon.
It made me remember the story of Noah
  and the Flood.
Thank you for the rainbow, Lord.

# Travels

Dear Lord,
We're off on vacation tomorrow.
I'm so excited.
Thank you for holidays!

Dear Lord,
I'm glad that, even when we're far from home,
you're still with us.
Please keep us safe.
Amen

# Quiet times

Hush little puppy with your bow wow wow,
Hush little kitty with your meow, meow, meow.
Hush Mr Rooster with your cock-a-doodle-doo.
Don't you moo moo moo, Mrs Cow.
Hush, hush, hush.
Hush, hush, hush.
Somebody's talking to God right now.

Dear Lord Jesus,
Thank you for prayer time.
Thank you that we can talk to you about
anything,
anytime,
anywhere.

Dear God,
Thank you that
– with you –
I'm never alone.
Amen

Dear God,
Thank you that we can tell you our secrets:
things that make us happy;
things we worry about;
things we look forward to;
things we're scared of.
We can share all of them with you.
Thank you, Lord.

# Please, God

God, make my life a little light
Within this world to glow;
A little flame that burns so bright
Wherever I may go.

Heavenly Father,
Guard my little tongue today,
Make it kind while I play;
Keep my hands from doing wrong,
Guide my feet all day long.

Dear Lord, thank you!
You answered my prayer!
Things went all right today.
You really helped me, Lord.
Next time I won't feel so frightened.

# My friend Jesus

Jesus, friend of little children,
Be a friend to me;
Take my hand and ever keep me,
Close to thee.

With all that I do,
And all that I say,
Help me to walk
In Jesus' way.

# When I'm scared...

Dear Lord,
Sometimes I get lonely.
I'm too shy to talk to anyone.
I feel left out.
Please help me fit in and make friends.
I know you will always be my friend.
Thank you, Lord.

# All the people I love

God bless all those I love;
God bless all those who love me;
God bless all those who love those I love,
And all those who love those who love me.

Dear God,
Please love me,
Take care of me,
Bless me.

Please love my sister,
Take care of her,
Bless her.

Please love my brother,
Take care of him,
Bless him.

Dear Lord Jesus,
Thank you for cuddles.
Thank you for hugs and kisses.

Dear Lord, thank you
for giving me so much love.
Amen

Dear Lord Jesus,
I love my mummy and daddy.
I love my brother and sister.
I love my grandma and grandpa.
Please look after them.
Please don't forget to look after me too, Lord!

Dear Lord,
Great news!
My new baby sister is here at last.
She looks very small.
Her fingers are tiny.
I can't wait to play with her.
Please help her grow up fast, so I can.

Dear Heavenly Father,
Daddy has to work so hard.
We hardly ever see him.
Please help Daddy at work,
so he can come home earlier.
Then I can kiss him goodnight
before I go to sleep.
Thank you, God.

Dear Lord,
Sometimes my brother makes
me cross.
I get fed up with him.
Please help me love my brother
and get on better with him.

# God's wonderful world

For air and sunshine, pure and sweet,
We thank our heavenly Father;
For grass that grows beneath our feet,
We thank our heavenly Father.

Lord God,
You provide streams of water
in the hills and valleys.
Birds build their nests nearby
and sing in the trees.
With all my heart
I praise you, Lord!

Dear Lord,
Today we went to the zoo.
We saw lots of animals you made.
Giant elephants, whizzy lizards,
mischievous monkeys, gentle deer.
You made them all, God,
big and small.

Thank you, Lord Jesus,
For all the plants and animals
You've given us to share –
From the yellow daffodil,
To the grizzly bear.

# Sorry!

Dear Lord,
I'm sorry I was so naughty today.
Please forgive me.
Sometimes I find it hard to be good.
Please help me to be nicer tomorrow.

Lord, please forgive me.
Today I was unkind to my friend.
Help her to forgive me
when I tell her I'm sorry.

God, you are great.
You made the world and it's so good.
We're sorry that we have spoiled it.
Please help us to do better.
Amen

# Children, everywhere

For lonely children everywhere,
Who don't have anyone to care;
Lord, I pray that you will send
A loving, kind, and special friend.

Lord Jesus,
Please make my friend well.
Help the doctors and nurses
make her better.
Amen

# Birthdays

Thank you, Lord,
For people and parties,
For presents and cards,
For songs and games.
Thank you for cakes and candles.
Thank you for birthdays, Lord.

Dear Lord,
I had the best birthday party ever.
All my friends came.
They gave me lots of cards and presents.
I blew out all the candles on my cake in one puff.
Thank you for a wonderful birthday.

# Harvest

All good gifts around us
Are sent from heaven above.
Then thank the Lord,
O thank the Lord,
For all his love.

Now thank we all our God
With hearts and hands and voices;
Such wonders he has done,
In him his world rejoices.

# Christmas

Loving Father,
Help us remember the birth of Jesus,
So we may join in the song of the angels,
Share the gladness of the shepherds,
And worship with the wise men.

What can I give him,
Poor as I am?
If I were a shepherd,
I would give a lamb;
If I were a wise man,
I would do my part;
Yet what I can I give him –
Give my heart.

# Easter

There is a green hill far away,
Outside a city wall,
Where the dear Lord was crucified
Who died to save us all.

Lord God, we thank you for your love,
shown to us in Jesus Christ,
who was willing to die for us.

Loving heavenly Father,
We thank you for the new life
that we celebrate at Easter.
Amen

# At the end of the day

Hello God! It's me!
What a great day it's been.
Did you see everything I did today?
Of course – because you're God!
Thanks for being with me.

Dear God,
I did something wrong today.
You know what it was, God.

I'm sorry.
Please forgive me.
Thank you, God.

Dear God,
Did you hear me crying today?
I was sad.
Thank you for listening
When I'm not so happy.

Heavenly Father,
Sometimes I get cross inside,
and have a bad mood day.
I scream and shout and stamp my feet,
if I don't get my way.

I'm sorry for my bad mood, Lord.
I'm glad that, whether I'm good or bad,
You love me anyway.

Lord Jesus,
Thank you for everything good
that happened today:
For keeping me safe and well.
For fun with friends,
For what I learned,
For those I love.
Help me to sleep safely tonight.
Amen

Dear God,
Tomorrow is a very important day for me.
You know about it.
Please look after me tomorrow.
Thank you for listening, God.
I am not so worried now.

# Bedtime

Matthew, Mark, Luke, and John,
Bless the bed that I lie on.
Four corners to my bed,
Four angels around my head.

Dear Lord,
I like it when I lie in bed at night
and listen to the wind and rain.
I feel cosy and safe.
Thank you for my snuggly, warm bed.
Please look after all the animals
outside in the cold.
Find them somewhere safe and warm.

Dear Lord Jesus,
Please look after me at bedtime.
Sometimes I wake up in the middle of the night
and feel scared.
Help me to remember you are always with me
and that I don't need to be afraid.
I'm glad you're my friend.

As night-time comes creeping,
And children are sleeping,
God watches us, deep through the night.

So hush now, no peeping,
For God will be keeping
Us safe, till the new morning's light.

Jesus, tender Shepherd, hear me:
Bless your little child tonight;
Through the darkness please be near me,
Keep me safe till morning light.

All this day your hand has led me,
And I thank you for your care;
You have warmed me, clothed and fed me;
Listen to my evening prayer.

# Through the night

From ghoulies and ghosties,
Long-legged beasties,
And things that go bump in the night,
Good Lord deliver us.

The Lord is my shepherd;
I shall not want.
Amen

# The Lord's Prayer

Our Father in heaven,
May your name be kept holy.
May your kingdom come soon.
May your will be done here on earth,
just as it is in heaven.
Give us our food for today,
and forgive us our sins,
just as we forgive those who sin against us.
And don't let us yield to temptation,
but deliver us from the evil one.
For yours is the kingdom, the power,
And the glory,
For ever and ever,
Amen

# An old prayer

God be in my head,
And in my understanding;
God be in my eyes,
And in my looking;
God be in my mouth,
And in my speaking;
God be in my heart,
And in my thinking.

# Index of First Lines

All good gifts around us ........................ 58
*Matthias Claudius (1740–1815)*
As night-time comes creeping ................ 77

Dear God, Did you hear me crying today? 69
Dear God, I did something wrong today ... 68
Dear God, I feel like praising you ............ 7
Dear God, Please love me ..................... 40
Dear God, Thank you for giving us the
Bible ............................................... 23
Dear God, Thank you that .................... 31
Dear God, Thank you that we can tell you
our secrets ...................................... 32
Dear God, Tomorrow is a very important
day for me ....................................... 72
Dear God, You know all about me .......... 24
Dear Heavenly Father, Daddy has to work
so hard ............................................ 44
Dear Jesus, Please help me at school ....... 13
Dear Lord Jesus, I love my mummy and
daddy ............................................. 42
Dear Lord Jesus, Please help me to be
brave .............................................. 14
Dear Lord Jesus, Please look after me at
bedtime ........................................... 76
Dear Lord Jesus, Thank you for cuddles .... 41
Dear Lord Jesus, Thank you for prayer
time ............................................... 30
Dear Lord Jesus, We have this day only
once ............................................... 10
Dear Lord, Great news! ...................... 43
Dear Lord, I am starting my new school
tomorrow ........................................ 11

Dear Lord, I had the best birthday party
ever ................................................ 57
Dear Lord, I like it when I lie in bed at
night ............................................... 74
Dear Lord, I saw a beautiful rainbow this
afternoon ......................................... 25
Dear Lord, I'm glad that, even when we're
far from home .................................. 27
Dear Lord, I'm sorry I was so naughty
today .............................................. 51
Dear Lord, Sometimes I get lonely ......... 38
Dear Lord, Sometimes my brother makes
me cross .......................................... 45
Dear Lord, Thank you for music ............. 20
Dear Lord, thank you! ........................ 35
Dear Lord, Today we went to the zoo ...... 48
Dear Lord, We're off on vacation
tomorrow ........................................ 26

For air and sunshine, pure and sweet ....... 46
*Traditional*
For lonely children everywhere .............. 54
*Author unknown*
From ghoulies and ghosties ................... 79
*Traditional Cornish prayer*

Give me joy in my heart ...................... 8
*Traditional*
God be in my head ............................. 82
*Sarum Primer (1527)*
God bless all those I love ..................... 39
*From an old New England sampler*
God is great, God is good ..................... 17
*Traditional*

God made the sun .............................. 19
God, make my life a little light................ 33
   *Matilda Betham-Edwards (1836–1919)*
God, we thank you for this food ............. 18
God, you are great ............................ 53

Heavenly Father, Guard my little tongue
   today ......................................... 34
Heavenly Father, Sometimes I get cross
   inside ........................................ 70
Heavenly Father, Thank you for our daily
   food .......................................... 16
Heavenly Father, Thank you for our school 12
Hello God! It's me! ........................... 67
Hooray! You made the giraffe as tall as
   a tree ........................................ 22
Hush little puppy with your bow wow
   wow ......................................... 28
   *Traditional*

Jesus, friend of little children ................. 36
   *Walter J. Mathams (1851–1931)*
Jesus, tender Shepherd, hear me ............. 78
   *Mary Lundie Duncan (1814–40)*

Lord God, we thank you for your love ..... 65
Lord God, You provide streams of water ... 47
Lord Jesus, Please make my friend well ..... 55
Lord Jesus, Thank you for everything good 71
Lord, please forgive me ....................... 52
Loving Father, Help us remember the birth
   of Jesus ..................................... 61
   *Adapted from a prayer by Robert Louis
   Stevenson (1850–94)*
Loving heavenly Father, We thank you for
   the new life ................................. 66

Matthew, Mark, Luke, and John .............. 73
   *Traditional*

Now thank we all our God.................... 60
   *Martin Rinkart (1586–1649)*

Our Father in heaven ........................ 81

Praise him, praise him.......................... 9
   *Traditional*

Thank you for the world so sweet .......... 15
   *Edith Rutter-Leatham (1870–1939)*
Thank you, Lord Jesus, For all the plants
   and animals .................................. 50
Thank you, Lord, For people and parties.... 56
The Lord is my shepherd ..................... 80
There is a green hill far away ................. 64
   *Cecil Frances Alexander (1818–95)*

What can I give him............................ 62
   *Christina Rossetti (1830–94)*
With all that I do ............................... 37